A SEED

of

HOPE

IN TOXIC SOIL

by Glenn Garvin

Former campers who are now adults have given us permission to use their names. In other cases, the names have been changed to protect confidentiality.

Royal Family KIDS, Inc.
3000 W. MacArthur, Suite 412
Santa Ana, CA 92704
714.438.2494
www.royalfamilykids.org

HOPE IS LIKE GOLD
IN THE ECONOMY OF
THE ABUSED.

Hope deferred makes the heart sick,
but a dream fulfilled is a tree of life.
— Proverbs 13:12 (NLT)

Table of Contents

Acknowledgments

My father God, who offered me the deal of all eternity: "If you'll give me your life, I'll be your Dad."

My wife, Robin, who took the brunt of my dysfunctional thinking and, through her love and patience, turned me around.

My children — David, Matthew, and Janae — who have each been a delightful dream and revealed a whole new future.

My father-in-law, Frank Triggs, for being a role-model and showing me how to be a great husband and father — without a manual.

My pastors and bosses, Wendell Vinson and Chuck Atherton, for taking a risk and allowing me to figure out my Christianity in community.

My mentor, boss, and friend, Wayne Tesch, who realized he has a niche for inspiring broken young men.

My friends, who have laughed when I wasn't funny, followed when I didn't know where I was going, and — most of all — believed in me.

Introduction

The Transformation Business

Glenn Garvin's life has been very different from mine. The relationships I had with my parents were strong; the relationships he had with his — all five of them — were broken. My hopes and dreams were encouraged; his were dampened. My worries and fears were alleviated; his were proven valid. I wanted a new bike; he wanted an adult to offer positive affirmation. I look back on my childhood with a wistful smile; he looks back on his grateful that it's in the past.

It would be reasonable for you to wonder how two men with such dissimilar backgrounds and experiences came to be friends and advocates of the same ministry, Royal Family KIDS, more than 20 years ago. The answer is simple: the life-transforming power of a loving God.

My dream of starting Royal Family KIDS Camps began in 1985 while I was serving as Senior Associate Pastor of Newport-Mesa Christian Center in Costa Mesa, California. Though our church had been sponsoring many successful summer camping programs for the children in our congregation and community, we realized that a significant group of kids was completely left out of the camping experience. The children in the Social Services system — foster children coming from despairing situations of abuse, abandonment, and neglect — weren't afforded the same opportunity to develop life-long connections with Christian adults and friendships with other students at a summer camp.

In 1985, the congregation of Newport-Mesa Christian Center partnered with me to change this, extending hands of compassion and offering hope to children in desperate need of both. That first summer of Royal Family KIDS Camps dramatically touched the lives of 37 foster children. As we began to see the difference one week of Camp could make — a chance for the kids to experience caring and respectful interactions with adults, create happy and positive memories full of fun and laughter, and find hope for a brighter future — it was clear that camps like this were needed all over the country.

A few short years later, Life Center — a church in Lakewood, California — heard about the important work we were doing, and they asked to launch the second Royal Family KIDS Camp using our model and materials. This is where Glenn comes in. As Associate Pastor of Life Center, he was deeply involved in establishing the Life Center Camp and directed that Camp for the next 10 years.

Eventually, Glenn joined our national office staff as Director of Mission Fulfillment. He speaks across the country, sharing stories of healing and restoration, and recruits churches to start Royal Family KIDS Camps that will meet the needs of foster children in their area. Today, we're extremely thankful to have impacted the lives of 72,795 children to date, and through 181 camps in 34 states, as well as 24 international Camps in 11 different countries, last year alone. And, by God's grace in 2012, we hope to start 20 more Camps and 12 more Mentoring Clubs that will serve these deserving children.

Over the course of Glenn's involvement with Royal Family KIDS, we have worked together and come to know each other as friends. Mentoring him in his various roles, developing our friendship, and witnessing his passion to help these at-risk children find hope, I have come to understand two very important things about Glenn.

First, though he and I have incredibly different pasts, we have the most significant things in common: We have both been saved by the grace of a loving God; we have both had His real and specific calling placed on our lives; and we have both been transformed by Him, forever changed.

Second, *because* he and I have incredibly different pasts, he is able to reach out in ways that I can't, to minister to a group of children we both care so deeply for — foster children coming from troubled situations similar to his own.

In this book, you will read some of Glenn's recollections of his childhood and the transformation that has taken place in his life. I have had the privilege of seeing firsthand the results of that transformation. I have watched him grow and become the man God has called him to be. I have watched him relate to children of Royal Family KIDS and understand them in ways that very few others are able to. I have watched him coach the Counselors and Volunteers, helping them to become effective beacons of love. I have watched God taking the brokenness of Glenn's childhood and creating something beautiful from the rubble — hope.

Based on eight of Glenn's sermons, the stories on the pages that follow will show you that God is in the business of transforming. He has been in this business for more than 2,000 years, making a spokeswoman out of the troubled woman at the well, a messenger of hope out of the man possessed by a legion of demons, and a giant-slayer out of a scrawny shepherd boy named David. God was in this same business as, little by little, Glenn found the strength to overcome his dysfunctional past. God did it through a "well done" from someone named Stan, a dinner prayer with Frank's dad, and an invitation to church camp from Thelma. God continues to be in the same business today at Royal Family KIDS — giving a boy who wouldn't speak a word the confidence to sing a song with the choir ... offering a birthday present to a young boy who had never received one before ... and providing a parentless young girl with a Royal Family. If God can do it for them, He can do it for anyone.

I trust you'll be greatly encouraged by these amazing stories of hope, healing and restoration! Thank you for sharing the vision of Royal Family KIDS, and helping to make so many of these stories possible.

— Wayne Tesch
Founder, Royal Family KIDS

CHAPTER 1

Moments Matter

love
Seeds of HOPE

I t was only a moment,
but it was a moment that
changed my life.

As I rode my hand-me-down
bicycle — complete with long
handlebars and a banana seat — down
the sidewalk of my neighborhood one
day, the chain fell off of the sprocket. I
got off of the bike and stared at the loose
chain for a few minutes. I suppose I was

hoping to fix it with the power of my mind. I didn't know much about fixing bikes at eight years old.

A voice called out to me, "Hey, do you need some help?"

I looked up and saw Stan, a retired neighbor from a few doors down. Stan and his wife, Louise, were the original owners of their house on Harding Street, and Stan spent all of his time meticulously perfecting every aspect of his property. He manicured the grass on his front lawn weekly, ensuring that it stayed the deepest shade of green with every blade standing at attention. He touched up the paint on his house, bright white with forest green trim, every year. Seeing how spotless he kept the outside, I could only imagine what the inside looked like.

I couldn't pass up his offer — after all, I had no idea what to do with a loose bike chain. Stan walked my bicycle up the driveway and into his garage. It was one of those garages that any man would love to call his own. The cement floor was so flawless it practically shone. No oil, scuffs, or dirt anywhere! The walls were lined with beautiful cabinets. A peg board held shiny tools hanging in order, an outline of each tool carefully drawn around every single one. Everything was in its place, hanging perfectly and ready for use.

Stan picked up the bike and skillfully flipped it on its back. After pulling the half-inch, open-ended wrench out of its position on the pegboard, he began to loosen the nut that held the back tire in place. He carefully untangled the chain, paused, and smiled. I could tell that he was about to impart to me the ancient wisdom of bicycle mechanics.

"Do you know about the 'master' link?" The way he asked the question made me feel like I was about to become privy to top-secret information. I looked both ways and over my shoulders before giving him the nod to tell me more. He continued in a hushed, reverent tone, "This is the 'master' link. It's the one link that will allow you to take the chain off to work on it."

"Wow!" I was mesmerized by the voice of this mechanical mastermind. *He's got to be the smartest man in the world*, I thought.

With the speed and skill of a seasoned craftsman, he re-assembled the chain around the sprocket. Just as he was getting ready to tighten the rear axle nut, he paused a second time. "You want to try it?" Stan extended the tool toward me and gently nudged me toward the bike.

I took the wrench in my hand. It felt good to hold it. It felt natural to hold it. It was as if, by holding that wrench, I held the joy of fixing something.

I began to turn the nut on the rear axle when Stan cleared his throat, indicating he had even more wisdom to share. "Turn it right to tighten, left to loosen — righty-tighty, lefty-loosey!" he exclaimed. "Put some muscle into it so it's on good and tight." I tucked away these secrets of the trade in my mind, wanting to remember his brilliance later.

Little did I know, Stan's tool-box secrets wouldn't be the most valuable words he shared with me that day. It was his next remark that would change my life, a moment that would forever transform Stan, a nice neighbor and bike-fixing genius, into Stan, my hero.

"You do that *well.*"

I looked around to see who else was in the garage. *Did he just say that to me?* I had to ask myself because I had never been told that I did anything well. I had four parents at the time (eventually I'd have five); not one of them told me I did something well. The birth mother I had never met didn't tell me. My biological father, a recovering drug addict who was in and out of my life without any pattern or consistency, didn't tell me. My adopted father, an alcoholic who took his own life when I was about twelve years old, didn't tell me. My adopted mother was too busy dealing with life to tell me. My fifth parent, a controlling and abusive step-father, didn't tell me I did anything well either, just for the record.

"You do that *well*."

It never struck me that he might just be trying to be kind. I mean, all I did was turn a lug nut on a bike axle — it wasn't like I put a man on the moon. I didn't care. I grabbed the compliment like a man in the desert grasping for a drink of water.

"You do that *well*."

I replayed those four words in my mind, over and over again. Those four words empowered me. From that moment on, I knew that I had the power to fix stuff. Those four words inspired me to greatness. I believed, if I could fix a bike, maybe there were other things I could fix. These four words left an impression on me for the rest of my life.

I cannot exaggerate the influence of four words.

I cannot overstate the power of a moment.

In one moment, God can change a life. In one moment, a wounded heart can begin to find healing. In one moment, hopeless situations don't look so hopeless anymore. In just one moment at a well, Jesus uncovered a need, redeemed a past, and laid out a new future.

A Moment at a Well

Picture it: Jesus and His disciples travel across the desert as they make the trip from Judea to Galilee, in John 4. The midday sun has been beating down on them, and they're tired and thirsty. As they pass through the Samaritan town of Sychar, they come upon a well. Jesus is particularly beat, so He decides it's time to take a breather.

Moments after the disciples go off to find food, a woman from the village of Sychar was making her usual trip to the well. She's been up and down the path to the well hundreds of times. For her, this chore was a mundane one — a constant trip, a constant drip. Her routine was regular. Her route was unremarkable. She also came to the well tired and thirsty — just a different kind of tired and thirsty. She was tired of life as she knew it and thirsty for a purpose.

Jesus asks the woman for a drink.

The woman is shocked. In those days, guys like Jesus didn't have anything to do with women like her. Though men had certainly asked *many* things of her, I suspect Jesus made His request differently — with kindness.

As Jesus invests just a few moments in conversation with a friendless woman at a well, He quickly finds a spiritual thirst within her. He challenges her beliefs about God and about herself. He offers her a different kind of water that quenches perfectly — water for the soul.

Just as He gets her interested in what He's offering, He pulls a Dr. Phil. "Let's bring your husband out here ..." And then — this isn't in the Bible, but — I think there would have been a long, awkward pause. Questions must have flooded her mind.

Maybe the truth was too painful or embarrassing, but she decides to tell Him a fraction of the truth. Not the whole truth, just enough to explain why she can't produce a husband — she has no husband.

Jesus isn't fooled. He fills in the blanks she's too embarrassed to fill in herself. She's gone through five different husbands, and the man she's with now is not her husband. Now if that isn't Dr. Phil-style Jesus, I don't know what is.

I would think that most women in this situation would have turned on their sandals and stormed off with a "how-dare-you-judge-me" glare. This woman didn't. No, this woman sticks around, and actually does something equally shocking — she argues with the Son of God. That took some guts! After speaking truth into this lonely woman's life, He reveals to her that He is the Messiah she has longed to see!

The disciples file in, puzzled as to why Jesus is in a conversation with a Samaritan woman. The woman, so excited to have met the Messiah, leaves her bucket behind and runs back to her neighborhood with a fresh slice of hope to share.

One moment at a well made the difference. The Samaritan woman arrived as a lonely outcast on a mundane trip for water; she returned as Sychar's first missionary with new purpose in life.

One moment is all it takes to spark a transformation.

One moment is all it takes to create someone's new beginning.

One moment spent cheering someone along. One moment building trust. One moment meeting an unspoken need. Every summer, moments offered by Royal Family KIDS Camp Counselors have changed the lives of foster children across the country.

Three Moments at Royal Family KIDS Camps

Jeremy wouldn't talk. Not just to adults. Not just to people he didn't know. He had been so severely beaten by his father that he just quit speaking. To anybody. He also wore a baseball cap so low on his head that no one could see his eyes.

On Wednesday, the campers played a game of kickball. It took a long time to get Jeremy to even consider playing, but — after some serious encouragement and coaxing — his Counselor convinced Jeremy to take a turn at the plate.

Hearts stopped when he missed the first kick. His Counselor was sure he would get discouraged and quit on the spot. He didn't.

As the second ball came rolling in, the Counselor prayed "Please, God. Help him to kick that ball!"

BAM!

Jeremy's foot soundly connected with the ball, sending it soaring into the outfield. Jeremy started running toward first base. The entire Camp cheered wildly. He hit second. The cheers grew louder. He made it to third. The cheers grew louder still. As Jeremy started the final sprint toward home plate, he decided to go all out and slide into victory.

WHOOSH!

With a cloud of dust and an eruption of cheers and applause, Jeremy slid face-first into home. His Counselor was right there in a catcher's crouch, cheering the camper on. Immediately, Jeremy got up and gave his Counselor a wide grin. "I've never scored a point before in my whole life!" Through tears of joy, his Counselor congratulated him on his all-star homerun.

Jeremy spoke a few more times after that. His hat started riding a little higher on his head, too. The greatest joy, however, came on Friday when all the kids sang for the adults. Jeremy's mom was in the audience as Jeremy belted out the words to a song he learned at Camp. His face, now fully visible beneath his cap, was beaming as he sang.

One moment of encouragement from a Counselor gave a boy who wouldn't speak the courage to sing.

Kevin had a lot of fears. It was understandable — he had been abandoned by his parents and had a hard time trusting anyone. He was just trying to get through life.

On the first day of Camp, Kevin's Counselor asked him if he wanted to go fishing. He quickly answered, "I don't like the water."

Kevin's Counselor didn't push the issue; he offered to let Kevin wear the life vest on land just to see what it felt like.

The next day, Kevin's Counselor suggested a walk by the water's edge — with the life vest on of course. Kevin was reluctant, but he liked his Camp Counselor. He felt safe enough with him to play in the sand at the shoreline.

The next day, Kevin's Counselor wanted Kevin to meet the fishing instructor. He was a retired fishing captain. Everyone at Camp knew him as "Captain Sea Wolf," but in his normal life he was just plain Sven. Kevin, again, reluctantly agreed to go out by the water.

Kevin and his Counselor slowly inched out to the dock. Captain Sea Wolf gave everyone a friendly greeting and persuaded Kevin to try holding a baited fishing pole. He showed Kevin how to cast a line and gave him assurance to try casting his own. Kevin hurled the baited hook into the water — and immediately proceeded to fall headfirst into the water after it.

Kevin came face-to-face with his biggest fear as he entered that water, but — almost as quickly as he fell in — Captain Sea Wolf was there to pull him out. He was safe near the water with Captain Sea Wolf and his Counselor around. Kevin didn't need to worry anymore; he could trust them.

As Captain Sea Wolf plopped a shivering, stunned Kevin on the end of the dock, the Counselor noticed that Kevin was still clinging to his fishing pole. To everyone's surprise, there was a fish on the end of Kevin's line! I think God had an angel put it there. I'm sure you can imagine where Kevin wanted to spend the rest of his week — fishing with Captain Sea Wolf.

Moments spent earning a young boy's trust turned a fear of water into a love of fishing.

A Royal Family KIDS Camp tradition started when Jason overheard me talking to my wife, Robin, about a birthday I had coming up.

"Hey, I have a birthday this week too!"

"Really? What's your favorite birthday memory?" I asked. "Did you get a special present? Did you go somewhere? Did someone throw you a party?" I'll never forget his answer.

"I've never had a birthday party."

One of his foster brothers was listening to our conversation. He snapped back, "You have so! Remember the time 'they' took you to Jack in the Box? That was for your birthday."

"Oh yeah," Jason admitted, "I did go to Jack in the Box once for my birthday."

I stood there in shock for a moment. *Is it possible that the only celebration of this boy's life is a fast-food hamburger?* The injustice of such an offense made me even angrier as I reflected on all the disappointments of my own past. I didn't have that many positive memories of my own, but I was determined to create one for this boy. I just couldn't let him go through another birthday without a present or a party.

I drove to the local Kmart and found a watch to give to Jason. As I was getting ready to check out, I told the cashier the story behind the watch. Through tears, she called her manager over to hear the story. The manager told me through tears of her own to just take the watch, no charge.

When I returned to Camp, I told Robin about my conversation with Jason.

She wondered aloud, "Do you think that's happened in the other children's lives too?"

I started asking some of the other kids about birthday

memories that week and found that many had the same story. Two of those children didn't even know their own birth date.

That's when Robin came up with a great idea, a tradition we've upheld since 1988 at every Royal Family KIDS Camp: we celebrate every single child's birthday with an "Everybody's Birthday Party." All of the children at Camp come to a celebration with cake, party favors, decorations, and presents just for them.

One moment of conversation with a young boy resulted not only in his first birthday memories, but in first birthday memories for the thousands of children coming to Camp since.

One moment can reinvent someone's future.

One moment can mend someone's past.

One moment can be enough for you to find your new beginning. One moment can be enough for you to help someone else find theirs. One moment is enough for hope to shine through.

Making Moments

Moments, no matter how big or small, do matter. They matter to little boys who need a "You do that *well*" for tightening a lug-nut. They matter to hurting women at wells longing for a fresh start. They matter to kids at Camps who need a Counselor's love and encouragement to make happy, positive, life-changing memories.

Whether you need a transforming moment for yourself or need to be a hero in someone else's moment, be encouraged. If He can do it for me, He can do it for you. If He can do it through me, He can do it through you. Be ready. God can use any moment to bring about change.

CHAPTER 2

Get Well

Knowledge
Seeds of HOPE

Being sick is easy. Getting well ... that's the hard part. Sick may have its disadvantages — it can be disabling, painful, and inconvenient — but people don't have to do anything to stay sick. Nothing has to change. They can keep living exactly the way they've been living and wake up sick again tomorrow. Perhaps they can even learn to tolerate the illness, ignore it when they can and accommodate it when they must.

Getting well may help them to feel better in the end, but sometimes the process of change can be more painful than the sickness itself. Surgeries leave you sore. Doctor's visits can be uncomfortable.

Getting well can be an even more taxing process for those who have been sick for a long time. Not only must they get well physically, but they must also adjust their mentalities. After living for years as a sick person, it can be a challenge to think, act, or react as anything but a sick person.

Which is the predicament the man in John 5 finds himself in ...

Take a journey with me to the first century. Amidst the beautiful backdrop of the Roman colonnades, one might expect to find rich and famous Romans lounging by the multi-tiered pools and working on their tans. Instead, the would-be ritzy area has been occupied by multitudes of the poor and sick — people who have limped or crawled for miles in search of a miracle. For many, the pool of Bethesda is their last hope for healing.

Why are all of these people flocking to the pool? From time to time an angel of the Lord would come and stir up the water, healing the first person who came into the pool next. Angels of the Lord — as far as I've seen in Scripture — don't do anything insignificant, so my visual image is not of an angel putting his little toe in and gently stirring the water. I like to picture the angel "whooshing" in, the wind from his massive wings causing swells and waves.

On one of the covered porches lies a man who has been sick for 38 years — a lifetime in those days. Jesus is probably walking around on the pool deck, perhaps enjoying the view, when He spots this handicapped man. As I imagine it, Jesus kneels down next to him and whispers in his ear, "Do you want to get well?"

Does Christ's question catch this man off-guard? Does he not understand what Jesus is asking him? One would think this man's answer would be a resounding "Yes! Of course! I would love to get well." Instead, he bemoans the fact that he can't get into the pool fast enough to be healed.

This man isn't really looking for a miracle. He's just looking for a break ... looking for some help ... looking for a chance ... looking for hope. He can't comprehend the idea of ever actually being healed — for him, it's not even a remote possibility. His focus is squarely on a story he had heard about the water, not on being made well. Perhaps this man is thinking, *Look — it has taken me years to manage my handicap. I think I've got the hang of it now. Well? I don't need to get well. I just need someone to help me into that water.*

He has been a sick guy for 38 years. He knows how to be a "sick guy." He doesn't have a clue how to be a "healthy guy." What does it mean to get well? What does it mean to be healed? Those are scary questions when you don't know the answers; they are even scarier when you do.

Healing means change. Jesus says, "Grab your mat and walk home." The man gets up, grabs his mat, starts walking home, and then gets a ticket from the spiritual police for carrying his mat on the Sabbath ... because in those days, nothing considered to be "work" could be done on that day without penalty or judgment. He had spent 38 years as a law-abiding cripple, and now he's a walking lawbreaker. Everything is different. His body has healed, but he's still thinking like a "sick guy."

When God hands us our healing — no matter what kind of healing it is — it can be difficult to embrace it because we still think like sick people. We're comfortable as sick people. We like our sick surroundings. We enjoy hanging out with our sick friends. We are used to our sick schedule. We have a handle on our sick responsibilities. Being well? That's a whole new ballgame.

How do people who only know sick learn how to act healthy? They learn by watching healthy people act healthy. They learn by changing their thinking in positive ways. They learn by gaining new perspectives on situations that sickness corrupted.

Redeeming Christmas

It was Christmas Eve. We had a silver Christmas tree strung with blue lights in our living room. My adopted mother had worked frantically all day at the factory so that she could come home early and prepare for Christmas. My mom had finally gotten my two-and-a-half-year-old little sister to go to sleep, and it was my job to put a dollhouse together for her.

My mom worked hard to make sure that there were presents under the tree, though there were never very many for either of us. I knew that the dollhouse was my sister's "big gift" that year.

As an 11-year-old, I was excited to have something constructive to do. I was tired of waiting to see if my adopted dad would come home that night. Holidays are difficult for the families of alcoholics, and mine was no exception. My dad was rarely home for any holiday. He would drink away most of his paycheck and stay away from home. Of the Christmases that he was with us, I only remember him being sober for a couple of them. Every celebration was the same with my dad, and it never got any easier for my mom. She would try to hide her pain, but it was impossible. The shame was written all over her face.

I went to bed after finishing the dollhouse and wondered what "big gift" my mom had gotten for me that year. I figured that dad would probably stumble in at two or three in the morning and pass out on the couch. Two o'clock was about the time that the bar owners decided they'd taken enough money from saps like my dad and closed up shop.

My mom woke me up at eight o'clock the next morning to help her finish getting everything ready. My sister popped out of bed not long after. Watching her sleepy eyes take in the gigantic pink and yellow dollhouse, I couldn't wait to see what my "big gift" would be.

As we dug out the smaller presents from our stockings, I noticed that my mom was stealing glances at the clock. After all of our gifts had been opened — my "big gift" nowhere in sight — my mother broke the news to me.

"Glenn, your dad told me that he would take care of getting your gift this year. He seemed excited and sincere, so I agreed. He's let me down before, but I never thought that he would disappoint *you*. I'm so sorry. I don't have anything to give you." She stared at me for a long time, as if she were searching for understanding in my 11-year-old eyes.

I didn't know what to say. How could she trust a drunk with my present? I was trying to find a way to hide my sadness. I was crushed, but I didn't want her to see that. I told her that it was all right. What else could I say? We had both been ripped off. For the rest of the morning, I watched my sister play and forced myself to celebrate with her.

A little before lunchtime, my dad lumbered into the house. He was greeted with the fury of a mother whose son had been disappointed on Christmas morning. That conversation was colorfully sprinkled with a lot of cursing and yelling, so my sister and I went to hide out in my room. We just wanted to pretend that we were having a normal Christmas.

The next thing I knew, my dad stormed through my room with my mom in heated pursuit. He grabbed me — hard — by the arm and dragged me out of the house. I was glad my mother made me wear slippers that morning. He threw me into his van and sped off down the street. At least he was driving straight. Perhaps the fight with my mom had sobered him up.

Thankfully, we did not have to drive very far. We pulled into my dad's favorite bar — the Tiki Room. The place looked like a rat hole from the outside, and the large gravel-covered parking lot rarely held more than three cars. The inside probably didn't look much better, but it was too dark to tell.

As soon as we walked in, my dad got into a serious conversation with the owner. He pulled a wad of cash out of his business-card-stuffed wallet and counted off a number of bills. After smacking the money down on the bar, he unplugged a color television without even turning it off. He lifted the well-used, thirteen-inch set off of a grimy shelf and motioned for me to follow him.

We drove home more slowly than we had left. After pulling into the driveway, my dad snatched the TV and huffed into the house. He set it up on a table in my room, plugged it in, and said "Merry Christmas" on his way out of the house. My mom tried to follow him and yelled out the door after him, but he ignored her. I could hear him revving the engine all the way down our street.

It took a few minutes to make sense out of everything that had happened. My dad had barely kept his promise, but it could have been worse. My mom came in to talk with me, and I gave her a pleading look — the kind of look you give after bringing home a stray dog.

"Can I keep it?"

Mimicking my dad, she said, "Merry Christmas, son."

After receiving a gift like that from an earthly father who didn't know what he was doing, it became difficult for me to receive anything from anyone. I was sick. I knew that my dad was the epitome of lousy, but lousy was all I knew. My instincts told me that dads were supposed to do better — be better — but I wasn't entirely sure what that kind of dad even looked like.

Unfortunately, I didn't have role models in my life to take me under their wing and demonstrate how good parents treat their children. I had to discover most of that on my own. Borne out of a desire to do better — be better — myself, I'd come up with ideas and ask God to reveal those qualities to me.

Though I had begun to heal from my dysfunctional childhood, my thinking was still crippled. As an adult, Christmas and holidays were the most difficult times of the year. To me, holidays represented pain — crushed hopes and broken promises. By God's grace, with the help of my patient wife, Robin, and an enlightening message on a Christian radio broadcast, the painful holiday seasons of my life became redeemed. I began to see that Christmas actually represented the very opposite of what I had experienced — the fulfillment of a Father's promise to send a Savior.

Getting well isn't easy. It's difficult for people to become healthy when all they've seen is what *not* to do. It helps to have someone pushing them along. It helps to have an encourager. It helps to have someone pointing them in the right direction. It helps to have someone say, "Hey — see that gift? That's for you."

Restoring a Birthday at Royal Family KIDS Camps

Robert had never been to Royal Family KIDS Camp before. On the bus ride, Robert overheard a discussion between a couple of the boys who had gone last summer. They were excited about a surprise birthday party with presents for everyone. Robert was curious and skeptical — no one had ever given him a present before.

"Is that really true? They have a birthday party? With presents for *everybody*?"

"Yeah! It's a huge party. They celebrate all of our birthdays. We get cake, presents, and everything! It's so much fun."

Robert wasn't so sure. Throughout the week, Grandma Ginger — a Volunteer at the Camp — observed Robert dejectedly repeat to himself, "I'm not gettin' no present."

The night of the surprise birthday party arrived, and Grandma Ginger looked forward to seeing Robert's face as he received his gift. Just to make sure that she got a good seat, she sat right next to him at the party.

The party coordinators started calling out children's names, and Grandma Ginger could hear Robert mumbling to himself, "I'm not gettin' no present." As each child went forward, Robert seemed to get increasingly depressed. "I'm not gettin' no present," he repeated.

Robert's name was finally called. Grandma Ginger's face lit up in excitement as she turned to Robert, but Robert didn't move. He didn't acknowledge hearing his name at all. His name was called a few more times, but Robert still didn't move.

Grandma Ginger couldn't take the suspense anymore, so she prodded him. "Robert? That's you! Go get your present!"

Robert slowly dragged his body over to receive his gift. He didn't seem excited at all. When he returned to his seat, he didn't bother opening his present. He just stared at it.

After a few moments, Grandma Ginger said, "Go ahead, Robert. You can open it now!"

Robert could not bring himself to open the gift.

"Robert, that present is for *you*. Don't you want to see what it is?"

"Do I get to keep it? Do I get to take it home with me?"

"Yes, Robert. *Now* will you open it?" Grandma Ginger said with strained patience.

Robert took a deep breath and said, "I think I want to open it later, back in my cabin."

Grandma Ginger told me it was then that she realized just how wounded so many of these little ones are.

Robert's Counselor later told us what happened when Robert returned to the cabin. He sat on his bunk and quietly opened the gift. He took things out one at a time, looking in wonder at each item. He carefully placed each present in the box when he was done, making sure that everything went back to its exact spot. With the lid firmly on the box, he slid it under his pillow for safekeeping.

How do children like Robert — children who only know "sick" — learn how to act healthy? They need to have someone like Grandma Ginger to show them ... to prompt them to get their gifts ... to be excited for them and with them ... and to assure them that the gift is theirs to keep.

Spreading the Cure

Getting well isn't easy. Everything changes. The way we lived when we were sick must be different from the way we live once we've been healed. Particularly for those who have only known sickness, it is important to find a support system of healthy people who can be encouragers and positive examples worth emulating.

Maybe you recognize your own need to be made well; or you may feel called to be a model of healthy living for someone else. No matter where you're at today, rejoice! Though getting well certainly isn't an easy journey, it is well worth it.

CHAPTER 3

All for One

L iving in a house of violence, I spent most of my childhood feeling terrified. The perpetual warzone that was my home life deeply disturbed and troubled me, leaving scars to uncover and discover for years long afterward. The yelling, cursing, drunkenness, and fighting always escalated, and it never ended well.

One horrifying incident in particular remains etched in my memory. It was a Friday night, and I stayed up a little later than usual to watch a movie with my adopted mom. My two-and-a-half-year-old sister was asleep in her crib. Mom and I heard a commotion coming from the front porch, and then the doorknob began to turn. My adopted dad had come home drunk. Again.

I froze. I wanted to run to my hiding place — a shuttered closet in one of the bedrooms. I'd go to that closet any time I was particularly upset or scared. Sitting on a pile of laundry and watching the light shine through the shutters felt peaceful. It always seemed to me that I escaped in that closet for just a few minutes, but my mother later told me the disturbing truth: I'd stay hidden away, staring at the shuttered doors, for hours on end. Terror runs deep.

Normally, my dad would start a major fight with my mom the minute he walked through the door. No matter how it started, it would quickly escalate to cursing and throwing things. But this night was different.

This time, he just mumbled to himself as he stumbled through the door. His shaky legs carried him right past both of us. It was as if he didn't even know we were there. My heart raced and my breathing was shallow until he left the room. *Whew! That was close.*

I began to relax and enjoy the movie again, but my mom remained tense. A few minutes passed, and she turned to me with a finger in front of her mouth and terror in her eyes.

"Shhh," she whispered. "Did you hear that?"

I shook my head. I hadn't heard anything, but I could tell that she had.

She whispered again: "Dad's loading his gun!"

I didn't even know my dad had a gun. As a child, I didn't fully understand the situation at home. All I knew was that, if my mom was scared, I should be scared too. Mom didn't waste any time. When he loaded that gun, it was the last straw. She realized that my dad was dangerous; she feared he might hurt me, my sister, her, or even himself.

"Get out of the house! Go next door. Have Francis call the police. I'll be right behind you with the baby."

I didn't hesitate. I ran out of the house barefoot. I only had my pajamas on.

The rest is all a blur. My mom and little sister came out shortly after. It seemed like it took forever, but the police finally arrived. Two police cars pulled right up onto our front lawn, and they talked with my dad for quite awhile.

That night my aunt came to pick us up, and we slept at her house. The next day, we were off to my Grandma's house in Arizona. We left my dad for good, and I never went back to that house again. We never talked about what happened. I finally felt safe, but there were still deep scars and real pains that I carried around with me for years.

For individuals — especially children — who go through abusive situations and experience traumatizing terror, the resulting psychological wounds tend to fester in silence. These secret hurts often have serious consequences. Helping these broken people begin to heal from their wounds — an extreme life-transformation — starts with something small. It starts with ministering to the one you can reach. Providing one shoulder to cry on. Giving one comforting embrace. Having one conversation. Offering one listening ear.

Comforting One at Royal Family KIDS Camp

Kelly came to Camp for the first time when he was 11 years old. He was a big kid for his age, but he was also very quiet. He just kept to himself for the most part.

The second evening of Camp, Kelly's Counselor, Dave, came to me with a big problem. Kelly had already been in two fights that day. He had also begun threatening to kill his fellow campers — and even some of the Counselors — when they got home from Camp. I took his threats seriously and had a talk with Kelly that night.

Kelly practically boiled with anger and rage. I did most of the talking, as he refused to even look me in the eyes. He kept repeating his threat from earlier in the day: "I'm gonna kill all of you!"

The next morning, Kelly was our first priority in the Staff prayer meeting. At lunch, Dave pulled me aside to talk. He had discovered where all of Kelly's anger was coming from, and it put everything into perspective. Just a few weeks before coming to camp, Kelly had been through a tragedy that would change his life forever. Kelly's dad, in a fit of rage, had taken out a gun and shot his wife in the head. Kelly witnessed the entire event. In a few terrifying moments, Kelly's mom was murdered and his dad was taken away.

For the remaining days of Camp, Dave spent most of his time simply listening to Kelly. The fighting stopped. The anger died down. Things seemed to get better. We survived the week, and I was more than relieved.

The next year, Kelly joined us for another week of Camp. When I saw him saying goodbye to his foster parents in the church parking lot, I wasn't sure what to expect. Kelly surprised me. He greeted everyone with a huge smile. On the bus, I overheard him telling first-time campers how much fun they would have. Kelly wasn't the same kid, and it showed every day.

A few nights later, at the surprise birthday party, I noticed that Kelly was quietly sitting by himself. It seemed unusual because he had been enjoying himself all week. I sat down beside him to talk.

"What's on your mind, Kelly? Is something wrong?"

Kelly quietly said, "This is my last year to come to Royal Family."

"I know." I paused. "Can I ask you a strange question?"

"Sure."

"Let's say I'm walking down the street in your neighborhood a few years from now, and I see you coming toward me. What kind of young man will I see?"

He didn't even hesitate. "You'll see a godly young man."

At that moment, I knew God had done a miraculous work in Kelly's life. He came to Camp an angry, resentful boy. One year later, he grasped what God was doing in his life. Because Dave had ministered to the one he could reach, a boy who had been marked with terror and bitterness could now see his own future as a "godly young man."

Jesus Himself ministered to the one — or rather "ones" — during His time here on earth. He offered freedom to those who were bound. He released those who were afflicted. He provided comfort for those who were terrified.

Releasing One

Climb aboard the boat found in Mark 5. After a night of toiling with the wind and the waves, Jesus and His disciples tie up their vessel on the shore of Gerasenes. It's getting late, and the moon's reflection on the craggy cliffs reveals hundreds of whitewashed tombstones. The exhausted disciples look around in confusion — why would Jesus bring them here?

What's that? One of the tombstones seems to be moving. A pale figure comes flailing down the hillside. Whatever it is, it's screaming and shrieking like a wounded animal. As the thin creature makes its way to the sandy shore, it becomes clear that this "thing" is actually a man. The filth and scars covering his body nearly camouflage his nakedness.

This man has roamed the graveyard for months, perhaps even years. He runs through the hills, day and night, cutting himself with sharp rocks. The villagers, taking pity on him, had tried to tie him up, but he would break the chains and shred the ropes. Those neighbors have given up on the man, believing no one is strong enough to tame him.

As he flings himself into the sand, he wails, "Son of the Most High God, I beg you not to torture me!"

"What is your name?" Jesus asks.

"My name is Legion," the pure evil within him answers. Within this man lives an army of terror — 6,826 demons. Jesus doesn't even flinch at the overwhelming number.

Rather than be cast away forever — banished to the Abyss — the demons make an odd request. "There's a herd of two thousand pigs over there. Send us into them."

Two unbelievable events occur in that moment.

First, the pigs start going nuts. They snort at the sky, shake with seizures, and run around frantically. With no warning, one pig leaps over the edge of the cliff. Within seconds, other pigs follow. Soon, the whole herd starts plummeting down the rocky embankment and into the sea below. With each thud-thud-splash, the pig-farming villagers — many of whom had tried to help the man before — grow more furious. As the local economy crashes before their eyes, they ask Jesus to leave.

Second, and more importantly, the man is released from the demons that have been terrorizing him. Now he can see the enemy's plan. Now it all makes sense. Free of the forces that had driven him to scream wildly, shred his shackles, and mutilate his skin, he can think clearly. The fog of death is gone, and the brilliant light of freedom reveals the truth. Christ sends the man back to his hometown to tell his story. Imagine hearing that testimony: "Let me tell you about the time I had 6,826 devils for roommates ..."

Christ intentionally made a trip to Pig Island on behalf of one very tortured man. He ministered to the one. He rescued a man — an irritant to the local community — from thousands of voices that urged him to kill himself. Though none of the villagers who tried to assist this one could help him, Christ was able to fill in that gap. Those villagers — unable to see the value of one homeless man in comparison to their lost money — sent Jesus and His weary disciples away, but Christ considered him worth the trouble. This man — abused, terrorized, and frightened for so long — finally found freedom through Jesus Christ.

Finding the One

Maybe you're going through a frightening situation right now. Maybe you've survived one. Maybe, like me, you've been carrying around secret scars and deep pain. Maybe, like Kelly, you're hanging on by a thread, waiting for someone to comfort you. Maybe, like the demon-possessed man, no neighbor or friend has been able to truly help you overcome your afflictions.

No matter where you are today, may your heart be lifted. Christ is able to fill in those gaps for you — tending your hidden hurts, comforting your broken heart, and healing what no one else can touch.

Maybe you know someone going through a scary time. Maybe your friend's situation seems impossible — too big for what you might say or do to change anything. Allow Christ to minister through you to reach the heart of that one. You can be used by God to bring comfort and healing to the fearful, broken ones in your life.

CHAPTER 4

Waiting for Providence

I thought this pit was my lot in life.

One night, when I was about 10 years old, my adopted mom was very agitated. It was getting late, and my adopted dad still hadn't come home from work. Not that it was unusual — he often went to a bar before coming home.

After a little while, my mom had had

Confidenc
seeds of HOPE

enough. She picked up the phone and started calling all of my dad's favorite bars. She'd ask for some of the bartenders by name and beg them to tell her where Dad was.

One of Dad's preferred hangouts, The Tiki Room, was pretty high up on Mom's list. After spending several minutes on the phone with the owner, Mom was absolutely convinced that Dad was there. She repeatedly asked the owner to put my dad on the phone, but he refused to help her.

Furious, my mom yelled into the phone, "We'll just see about that!"

Dad was dangerous when he was drunk. He had already caused a few wrecks and had a number of DUIs. One time, after hitting a car full of guys, he was followed home, beaten, and left unconscious on our front lawn. Mom had been trying to figure out a way to be more proactive about the situation. We couldn't let Dad drive drunk again. Who knew what would happen next time — he could wind up on someone's front lawn or wrapped around a telephone pole.

Now, slamming the phone down, Mom grabbed her purse. "I'm going to go 'steal' Dad's van," she said. "I'm not gonna let him hurt someone."

It was scary and exciting at the same time. I mean, stealing my dad's van while he was drinking in a bar? I wanted to see that one. It was only a mile or so to The Tiki Room, so I offered to peddle my mom there on the handlebars of my bicycle.

I peddled down side streets, across the main boulevard, past a few storefronts, and into the gravel parking lot of the ratty bar. We quickly spotted Dad's van and proceeded to execute our secret mission. We put my bike in the back. Mom hopped into the driver's seat, and I slid in on the passenger's side. We were careful to leave the headlights off until we were on the street. Mission accomplished! Dad wouldn't be driving drunk that night.

Sadly, it was only one battle won, not the war. This scene — a pre-teen boy doing whatever he could to keep his alcoholic father from driving drunk — would play out twenty times or more during my childhood. This was my upside-down life. This was the insanity of my day-to-day existence. This was my slimy pit.

I thought that this pit was my lot in life. I knew that I needed to be rescued. But I knew I would never get out without some help. I clung to the hope that someone would eventually pull me out. At the time, I had no idea that there truly was a Rescuer who would climb down into my pit, bring me out, and set me on solid ground. I had to wait it out.

No one likes to wait. We search for the shortest checkout lines. We avoid traffic at all costs. We get annoyed when a friend arrives late to a coffee date. We use microwaves to speed up our ETE — Estimated Time of Eating. It's difficult to wait in everyday situations like these. It's even more difficult to wait when you're in pain.

Waiting for Shoes at Royal Family KIDS Camp

Disembarking the bus, Keith was excited about his first time at Royal Family KIDS Camp. Like many of the other kids jumping into Camp that week, sweet anticipation was written all over his face. He introduced himself to his Counselor, Mark, and began making himself right at home in his cabin.

As Mark and his campers went exploring the campgrounds over the next few days, he couldn't help but notice that Keith was walking funny. Mark asked if everything was okay, but Keith knew how to wiggle around the question.

While Keith was getting ready for swim time at the pool, Mark asked to see Keith's tennis shoes. It only took a second to discover why Keith had been having a difficult time walking. The size was clearly wrong, and the shoes were over-worn — the soles on the shoes were practically non-existent. There was no telling how long Keith had worn them.

As he inspected the shoes, Mark saw some names scribbled into what was left of the insole. Keith's name was fifth on the list. Four other boys had worn these shoes before Keith, and the shoes didn't even fit him. Mark nearly broke into tears.

Mark alerted a Camp Staff member, who bought Keith some new tennis shoes. Keith wouldn't have to walk in pain anymore — his wait was over. The new shoes were a perfect fit, and Keith's name would be the only one written inside.

Waiting on the Shepherd

No one likes to wait. No one likes to be trapped in a painful situation. No one likes to be stuck in the mud. No one likes to *need* to be rescued. However, when you're out of answers, out of time, out of money, out of options, and out of hope, it's nice to know that — if you wait on Him — the Rescuer will come to save you.

In Psalm 40, a psalm of memories, late in life, David recalls an all-too-familiar scene from his childhood — before the giant, the Kingdom, and his seven wives (seen in 1 Chronicles 3) ever came into the picture. He remembers the younger days, when he was just a shepherd boy looking after his flock.

How many times did one of his sheep wander off? How many times did one from his flock fall into a slimy, dirty pit? How many times did one from David's flock become trapped, unable to move and vulnerable to both predators and the elements? Sheep don't have a very impressive learning curve, so it probably happened a little too often.

As David reflects on his numerous sheep recovery missions, he remembers the sights, the smells, and the sounds. He sees a lamb buried up to its neck in thick, cement-like clay. He can smell the wet, muddy wool filling the air with a sense of desperation. He can hear the hoarse wails of a trapped lamb looking for help. Perhaps the bleating of a lamb, stuck and in need of its shepherd, triggers this powerful visual image of his own Rescuer:

> I waited patiently for the LORD;
>> he turned to me and heard my cry.
> He lifted me out of the slimy pit,
>> out of the mud and mire;
> he set my feet on a rock
>> and gave me a firm place to stand.
> He put a new song in my mouth,
>> a hymn of praise to our God. (Psalm 40:1-3, NIV)

When a sheep falls into a sinkhole, the job of a shepherd is to go in after it. He must stoop to reach under the body of the lamb so he can lift it out of the pit. Many times, the hole was so big that the shepherd would actually have to wade into the muck, pick up the lamb, and struggle back to firm land. There were probably many times when a lamb, ignorant that it was being rescued, would kick and bite the shepherd. The shepherd would ignore the resistance and save the lamb — not how it wanted to be saved, but how it *needed* to be saved.

It's the same with our Rescuer's love for us.

Love sees through the pain.

Love overlooks the obstacles.

Love gets dirty.

Love makes waiting worthwhile.

Waiting Together

Perhaps you've fallen into a deep pit. You can't seem to make it out yourself — the walls are too high, and there's nothing to hold on to. You see even greater danger coming close, ready to pounce while you're vulnerable. You've been waiting for someone to help you out of the mud for a while, or at least it feels that way. Don't lose heart — the Rescuer hears your cries. Though it may not be in your time or the way you'd like to be rescued, He will send help to bring you through.

Perhaps you know someone who is stuck in a ditch. Cry out to the Rescuer with them. Love and comfort them. Wait with them. If you're willing to get dirty, God can even use you to be a part of the rescue mission He has planned for them.

CHAPTER 5

Giant Killers Club

Growing up in the sixties, I was a child of the comic-book-hero resurgence. Because of these stories about ordinary people discovering super powers and utilizing them to rescue others, I wanted to be one too. I would doodle and day-dream about my own rescue operations — usually to save a cute girl in my class. By night, I would spend my last moments of consciousness flying, leaping, or putting myself in harm's way to be the unsuspected hero. I longed to be a hero all because I saw Batman and Superman do it first.

Everyone loves a good hero story. Something in each of us longs to see justice come to pass. We root for the underdog to succeed and the innocent to be rescued. When a hero steps up to an impossible task and emerges victorious, we celebrate with hearts full of awe and wonder.

The story in 1 Samuel 17 is no different. We all know — and many love — the heroic tale of David and Goliath. The scrawny shepherd boy, lacking in experience and strength, volunteers to face a giant the entire army of Israel is scared to challenge. The kid grabs five smooth stones, and the first one he tosses in his sling knocks the giant out cold. David kills Goliath with one tiny rock, and Israel is saved.

After hearing this story preached in sermons so many times, it's difficult to imagine that there are many different angles or new ways of considering the story. I know, I thought so. Imagine my surprise when, during a devotional time, I discovered that David wasn't the only Bible character to face off with a giant!

I once heard a pastor joke that the four extra stones David picked up weren't by accident — the spare rocks were in case Goliath had four brothers. I just thought it was a funny idea at the time, but now I know he wasn't far from the truth. Goliath did have a brother and three very large friends, and all four of them had one thing on their minds: Revenge!

Years later, in 2 Samuel 21:15-22, the Philistines are at war with Israel again. David and his men are smack dab in the middle of the action, and David is getting tired fast. Out of nowhere, a huge giant named Ishbi-Benob comes right for David. This giant, wielding a seven-pound spearhead and a brand-new sword, has David cornered. David thinks it's all over when, all of a sudden ...

Hold on. Let's rewind and watch the extended scene from David's first battle in 1 Samuel 17: There are other young men on the battlefield watching David achieve the impossible. As everyone shouts in victory around them, that moment is forever emblazoned on their hearts. A few of those young men think, *Someday, I'm gonna get me one of them giants like David did.* They long to be heroes all because they see David do it first. In fact, David started the first "Giant Killers Club."

Now back to 2 Samuel 21: The dreams of those men come true. It's a good thing, too, because David is in need of a few good men to get him out of a giant conundrum. In that first battle, Abishai rescues David from Ishbi-Benob. At another battle, Sibbecai takes down a giant named Saph. At the next battle, Elhanan kills Goliath's brother. In still another battle, David's nephew, Jonathan, slays a giant with six fingers and six toes.

As I read these stories about the other four giant slayers, it seems to me that David *did* pick up five stones for a reason. With one stone, David killed his own giant; with the other four, he showed some young men that it was more than possible and inspired them to greatness. These other four giant slayers never would have thought that they could take down giants had they not seen someone equally ill-equipped do it first. David didn't kill one giant on the battlefield that day; he killed five. We need heroes to defeat giants just to prove that it can be done.

Two of My Heroes

When I was nine years old, I was allowed to spend the night at my best friend's house. That evening, I went to Frank's in time for dinner. Dinner at his house was different. The whole family — which included me that night — gathered around the table together, and then everybody paused. They all reached out to hold hands, and Frank's dad said a simple prayer of thanks for the dinner.

I wasn't fully able to process what happened at the time, but that picture — a family praying together before a meal — stuck in my head. I told myself that if I ever had a wife and children, I would hold hands and have prayer with them. I held onto that thought until Robin and I had a family of our own. Just like Frank's family, we have prayer, and — from time to time — we even hold hands.

When I was seventeen years old, as Robin and I were dating, I spent a lot of time hanging out at her house. I was there one evening on a school night, and Robin's younger brother and sister were going to bed. Renee, already looking sleepy, came down in her jammies and shuffled over to her mom and dad. They said a quick prayer and kissed her goodnight.

Ron came down not long after. He went over to his mom and dad, said a quick prayer with them, and got his goodnight kisses too. As I watched that nighttime ritual, I was stunned. Robin's dad kissed Ron on the cheek and told him that he loved him. I had never seen a father kiss his son before. I also had never heard a dad share with his son those powerful words — *I love you.*

No one noticed my eyes pop out of my head or my jaw drop to the floor, but I asked Robin about it as I was leaving.

"What was that all about earlier?"

She had no idea what I was talking about. "What do you mean?"

"Your dad kisses your brother and says that he loves him?"

"Oh, he does that all the time."

Wow, and SNAP! A mental picture was taken. Dads can be affectionate with their sons and say nice things, like "I love you." *If I ever have a son, I'm going to kiss him and tell him that I love him.*

I have been triply blessed. Not only do I have a very lovable and kissable daughter, but I also have two sons. Without trying to embarrass my boys, I often kiss their foreheads and tell them, "*I love you.*" I owe that to Robin's dad.

I've had a lot of giants to kill in my life. Had it not been for a few heroes to show me how it's done, I really doubt that I could have figured out how to be a good husband and father. They left me with unforgettable snapshots of how families could be — how they should be. Those powerful pictures allowed me to see that it could be done and inspired me to try. We need heroes to defeat giants just to prove that it can be done.

Heroes at Royal Family KIDS Camp

One afternoon, I received a call from Marnie, a social worker who helps us bring kids to Camp. She had an update for me about one of our campers, Jonathan. As I remembered, he had a great time just being a kid at Camp.

What I didn't know was that Jonathan had some serious problems before coming to Camp. Marnie filled me in, explaining that he had been in therapy since he was three years old. He was full of anger, out of control, foul-mouthed, and he had attempted suicide multiple times. Jonathan had been in seven foster homes, and his current foster parents — longing to adopt him — were losing hope because they couldn't control him. How can you pack that much junk into an eight-year-old?

Marnie went on to tell me about Jonathan's therapy session after returning from Camp. The therapist couldn't believe the difference! Jonathan's attitude and behavior had completely turned around, and the therapist wanted to know what had happened since Jonathan's last session. Marnie told him that he had attended a week-long summer Camp.

The therapist wanted to know what we did at Camp that caused such a remarkable change, so Marnie called me to find out.

"What happened at Camp?"

I told her exactly what we did. "We simply loved him."

What moment did Jonathan take away from Camp? What snapshot of how life could be — how it should be — stuck in his mind? We don't know. But we do know that hope was born in his heart. Jonathan's Counselor, Andy, stepped up and conquered a giant for Jonathan — he showed him how to love and inspired him to do the same. We need heroes to defeat giants just to prove that it can be done.

Slaying Giants

Maybe you see people struggling in your life and want to tell them how to kill the giants in their lives. I'd urge you to go one better — show them. If you want to teach someone how to love their children, then love your children. If you want to teach someone how to control their anger and frustration, then control yours. It's very difficult for people to become giant-killers by reading how-to books, but — if they can watch someone living the life of a giant-slayer — they can believe it's possible. You too can be someone's hero, an inspiration to greatness.

Perhaps you have a giant in your life that seems too tough to handle. Maybe you've seen someone kill a giant and wonder if you can do it too. Please be encouraged! No matter how big the giant looks or how weak you feel, with God's help, you can be more than a conqueror. Look around to the family of God for inspiration — solid people, grounded in their faith, who can give you those mental pictures of how life can be. You never know — perhaps by stepping out in faith to kill the giant in your own life, God will use you to be that same inspiration for someone. When you are ready, just let me know. I'd love to personally welcome you into ... the Giant Killers Club.

CHAPTER 6

Game of Life

The Game of Life, a popular board game from the Milton Bradley Company, seems to exemplify the American Dream. By "spinning the wheel," we playfully ask ourselves many of life's important questions:

Should I go to college or go directly from high school to a trade job?

Should I get married?

Can I afford to get married?
Should we have kids?
How many kids should we have?
Can we afford a house?
What kind of car should we buy?

In the game's economy, the best answers come from landing on good squares — squares that cost minimally or pay greatly. In the game, the player living in Millionaire Estates and in possession of the most money at the end is viewed as the winner.

How does God view the game of life? Jesus gives us some insight. In each of His parables, we are given a glimpse of real life — Kingdom life. As in many of His other parables, Christ begins the story of Matthew 25:14-30 drawing a clear connection between common activities — like farming, fishing, celebrating, or doing business — and God's Kingdom in heaven.

In this vignette, Jesus likens God's Kingdom — God's determination of life's winners — to a businessman leaving on a trip. Before the businessman heads off, he gives three employees some money to invest for him while he's gone. To one, he gives the equivalent of 5,000 dollars. To another, he gives 2,000 dollars. To the third guy, he gives 1,000 dollars.

The businessman is gone for a long time, and when he returns he wants a report from each employee about the investments he made. The one who was given 5,000 dollars has doubled the boss' investment. The one with 2,000 dollars has done the same. The man who was given 1,000 dollars, having buried his money rather than investing it, hands back the exact amount of money he was given — no more, no less.

Though sticking 1,000 dollars in the ground like an old Hot Wheels car doesn't make much sense, this man's burying of his master's money isn't the biggest shock for me. No, the biggest surprise is *why* the man buried it.

"I buried it because you are a mean, harsh, and unfair boss!" the employee explains. "I buried it because I don't like this game — I'm not any good at it. I buried it because I was afraid of losing the money you gave me to begin with."

Wow! How would you like to have this guy handling your 401(k)?

"You are a lazy, wicked employee!" the boss replies. "Even knowing what I expected of you, you have done nothing! I could have put my money in a CD at the bank and gotten more interest!"

Shaking his head in disgust, he gives the 1,000 dollars to the servant who returned with 10,000 dollars. Before instructing security to escort this unprofitable servant off the premises, the boss makes his rules clear: "Whoever has money will be given more. As for those who have nothing to show for themselves, even that will be taken away from them."

Wait a minute! That's a picture of how God plays the game of life? This is how God determines the winners? The Kingdom of heaven is like what? Unfair and cruel?

The point of this story isn't simply about how we invest God's money, though that is a part of it. The point of this story isn't that God is a harsh, spiteful, and unreasonable judge, either. To see God as materialistic or brutish would be both a misperception of the Kingdom and of God Himself. God made His greatest investment in all of creation in *us*. Would it be completely unjust of Him to ask for a return on that investment? Can we really expect Him not to care how that investment gets spent?

The point of the story is to make us think. As the employees in God's business — the Kingdom of heaven — how are we participating? How are we investing in Kingdom stuff? God has given to each of us in varying amounts — talents, money, influence, and wisdom. With whatever it is that we have been given, how have we utilized it to increase the effectiveness of God's Kingdom? To put it bluntly, what is the R.O.I. (Return on Investment) from us?

Letting Go of "Third Guy Thinking"

Almost 10 years ago, Wayne Tesch asked me to go to a Directors' training seminar for Royal Family KIDS Camps at a Camp in North Carolina. From the time I transitioned out of directing the Camp sponsored by my church, Life Center, Wayne had been looking for a way to keep me involved. While we were in North Carolina, he offered me a full-time job at Royal Family's national office.

"I want you to come work for Royal Family," he said, "but I can't pay you."

This was the strangest job offer I had ever received.

"How am I supposed to live and take care of my family if I don't get paid?" I asked.

"You would have to raise your own support," he replied. "You would be a missionary to abused and neglected kids."

Off the top of my head, I couldn't think of a polite way to tell Wayne "no," so I told him I'd think about it. Robin and I had been staff pastors at one church for 18 years. I already had a full-time job, and I didn't have to raise my own salary and work budget to do it. Though I left Wayne with some hope, I had already made up my mind to turn him down.

That Sunday at the host church in North Carolina, we had a Royal Family KIDS Camp commissioning service. After preaching from Matthew on the parable about the businessman and the three employees, the senior pastor challenged the congregation with a comment that hit me right between the eyes: "You know, most Christians live their lives out of fear."

BAM! That was me. I had been arguing with God for months — long before Wayne made his offer. God would ask me to trust Him, and I would agree ... as long as it didn't involve change. He was patient with me, but He kept prompting me to let go of these pillar issues like safety and security. I couldn't say yes. After working so hard to claw my way out of an insecure life and an unsafe childhood, I refused to budge on these matters.

By the end of the week at training, Wayne had the idea to ask someone to underwrite my salary and budget while I raised support. I was sick. I also received a stern personal word from the same pastor who had shot me from the pulpit. I knew I was cornered. I had to pray a prayer that asked the question, *Should I go?* Have you ever prayed a prayer that you did not want answered?

Honestly, I was still willing to tell God "no." I didn't truly change my mind until He spoke to me during a time of prayer: "Son, I am not so concerned about your faith and growth in this area. However, I am concerned about your children. How will they know what it looks like to trust Me and live by faith if they don't see it in your life? Though you believe you're giving them safety and security, you're teaching them to trust in themselves."

That was it. He broke me, and I gave up. If God really wanted me to abandon everything I knew and follow Wayne's crazy plan, I would do it. I would jump off this cliff, with faith that He would catch me. "I was bought with a price," I mumbled to myself. "My life is not my own. I came to God with nothing. What do I have to lose?"

So here's the confession: I <u>was</u> that lazy servant. I <u>was</u> the third guy! I had been given something to invest, but my heart was full of fear. Spiritually lazy, I kept taking safe routes and comfortable paths. I kept hiding the resources God had given me because I didn't want to play in the "Kingdom sandbox." The truth of the matter was this: I didn't want to play because I didn't want to *fail*.

Participating in the Kingdom of heaven and investing the resources that God has entrusted to me has revitalized my entire life. I still struggle with my "third guy thinking," but I hesitate less and laugh at my failures more. Now, I am able to recognize when I am being paralyzed by fear, and I force myself to move forward. I am blessed to be able to see some of the fruit of my investment, and that fruit encourages me to keep going.

Investing in Royal Family KIDS Camp

Since we have been given so much, how do we pour it back into God's business? How do we participate in the Kingdom of heaven? What are the "Kingdom sandboxes" that God wants us to play in?

God's ultimate cause is for everybody to know His love, but Scripture points to some who have a special place in God's heart. That list — which includes widows, orphans, and the poor — is a long one, but I think one of God's favorite sandboxes is where children who have come from painful and abusive backgrounds receive love and care. The Kingdom of heaven benefits when we invest in the lives of disenfranchised children — children like Amy who have come through Royal Family KIDS Camp.

Amy was a 10-year-old with juvenile diabetes, a learning disability, and speech problems. Though she was in the fourth grade, she couldn't read, write, or do the simplest math problem. She had been abused by male family members, taken away, and put into a foster home. After a foster brother shot her with a BB gun, the state moved her back in with her mother — who sexually abused her. Her next two placements, an abusive foster home and a failed family placement, left Amy sinking through the cracks of the system.

She didn't have much hope until she attended Royal Family KIDS Camp. There she met a Camp Staff member who looked past her own fear. Questions like "How will I afford to care for a child with all of these special needs?" and "What happens if I fail?" were met with faith. That Staff member began the process of adopting little Amy. I imagine Amy has since become a legal part of that family. Because of one Staff person's commitment, as well as the investments in Royal Family KIDS made by people like you, Amy's life will never be the same.

Playing the Game of Life

The way God evaluates the winners is very different from the way the world does. When this game of life is over, it won't matter where you lived. It won't matter what car you drove. It won't matter how much money was in your bank account. What *will* matter is how you invested back into the Kingdom of heaven what you were given.

Maybe you've been given the talent to speak publically, heal patients, sing songs, run businesses, or write books. Maybe you've been given the money to invest in churches, shelters, missionaries, non-profits, or ministries like Royal Family KIDS. Maybe you've been given the influence to persuade, inspire, or empower others. Maybe you've been given the wisdom to advise, teach, counsel, or guide the broken. Whatever gifts you've been given — in whatever amount it has been given — pour it back into God's business. By investing in the Kingdom of heaven, you will reap rewards that bear fruit eternally.

A Seed of Hope in Toxic Soil

CHAPTER 7

Who is My Mother?

W hen I was seven years old, I received P.D. Eastman's best-selling children's book *Are You My Mother?* as a gift. It was my favorite book for a long time.

In the story, a mother bird's egg is about to hatch. The egg begins to rustle around, and the mother bird goes off to find her soon-to-arrive baby something to eat. The baby bird hatches while its mother is away, and he wonders where his mother is. The baby bird goes off to look for his mother but, not knowing what she looks like, walks right past her.

Perhaps the reason I loved this book so much was because I felt like that baby bird. I missed my birth mother. I didn't realize just how much until a few years ago.

I was at a Royal Family KIDS Camp Directors' training class. It was the first day of training. The room was full of interested people anticipating the opportunity to learn about changing the world: one abused child at a time.

A VHS training tape, "Multiple Transitions," began to play. The video was simple — a PowerPoint style slideshow with bold yellow words on a black background — but effective. The music accompanying the video — dirge-style bagpipes — set a very dark mood, perfect for the content. The information helped the adults to understand the difficulties faced by the kinds of children coming through Royal Family.

As the second slide popped up, a young child's voice could be heard over the bagpipes. I thought this was an effective touch. I'm a sucker for the voices of children — they're so honest. What the boy said really resonated with me: "When you're a little kid ... when you barely remember what your first mother smelled like ... "

It took me right back to the feelings I couldn't put words to or explain as a child. I realized that I didn't know some very important pieces of information about my birth mother. I didn't know what she looked like. I didn't know what her voice sounded like. I didn't know what she smelled like. I began to heave sobs. Somehow that little guy's voice and the yellow words in the darkness became a long-lost key to a door that had been locked for over 40 years.

Like the bird in the story, I missed a mother I had never known.

I have wondered if, like the bird, I ever passed her without realizing it. Unlike the bird, I never did find my mother. I actually found myself very jealous of that baby bird.

Before you start feeling sorry for me, don't forget — by God's grace, I did turn out okay. The topic of mothers has always brought about a sense of loss for me, like turning a page in the middle of a book and finding it blank. However, because of the shortcomings in terms of my own biological family, I have a greater appreciation for the family of God — the mother and father figures I've found in the Church.

Jesus' Family

In Matthew 12:46-50 and Mark 3:20-35, a peculiar little scene takes place between Jesus and His family. Jesus, hitting the peak of His popularity, is joined by a crowd as He dines at someone's home. Tension is heightening as Jesus continues to satisfy the needy and dissatisfy the self-reliant. The Pharisees are out to trip Him up.

Because of this tension, Jesus' family starts getting more protective of Him, and the Jewish community. His mother and brothers know that their safety depends on keeping a low profile with the Romans and the religious leadership of Israel — they have the power to arrest and kill instigators. Mary and the brothers hear about this big meal, and they show up, trying to persuade Jesus to be low-key and keep the miracles under wraps. The Gospel of Mark even says that they wanted to take charge of Christ — presumably to make Him stop.

Jesus is in the middle of teaching when His mother and brothers arrive with a message for Him. The context of the story doesn't give me the impression that this is unusual, but rather parenthetical. Perhaps Mary has interrupted Jesus before. The family waits outside of the house, instead having someone from the crowd take Jesus a message. Notice that they don't call on one of the disciples, just someone from among the ever-growing population of groupies. Perhaps the disciples are under orders to ignore His mom's controlling requests!

So the unofficial messenger says, "Hey Jesus, your family is outside. They seem pretty anxious to talk to you."

"Who is My family?" He responds. "Who is My mother or My brother?" Jesus takes a look around and points to the gathering. "This is My family. Whoever does the will of My heavenly Father is My family."

There are eternal purposes that include both a sense of urgency and risk. There are godly priorities that supersede the needs of a biological family. The term "family" has a much broader definition in God's eyes than simply a blood relation. The will of God calls us to inclusionary action and implores us to widen our circle of love — to encompass far more than our nuclear families.

Particularly when it comes to caring for, nurturing, and protecting children, we should apply this principle. Who are their mothers and fathers? We are. The Church — the people of God — become the parents of the parentless.

Providing a Royal Family

Shaunte, a seven-year-old girl, attended her second grade class at school. The teacher asked the children to prepare a show-and-tell presentation of their families for the next day.

Shaunte had a more difficult time coming up with a presentation than the other students. She didn't have a biological family to show-and-tell about. She didn't have an adopted or foster family, either. Shaunte lived in a group home.

After thinking long and hard about what she would share at school, Shaunte decided to bring in pictures of herself at Royal Family KIDS Camp. At the front of the classroom, she introduced each family member as her own. "This is my Grandma. This is my Grandpa. This is my Aunt. This is my Uncle. This is my Camp Counselor — she's like my big sister."

The children in the class began giggling as Shaunte pointed out each member of "her family." They were laughing because the family members were all Caucasians — and Shaunte is an African-American. Shaunte's teacher (who happened to be a staff member at a Royal Family KIDS Camp) tried to help out by telling the children not to laugh.

Shaunte didn't need any help. "I know they're not my 'real' family," she proudly explained. "They're better than a 'real' family. They're my *Royal Family*."

Shaunte is one of many children who come through Royal Family KIDS Camps, who don't live with a biological mother or father of their own. Each summer, we are able to answer those children's painful questions — "Who is my mother?" and "Who is my father?" — by telling them, for that week, *we* are. We bandage their boo-boos. We dry their tears. We show them they are the most important children on the planet. We smile and affirm them. We love them. *We* are their Royal Family.

Finding Family

Perhaps you can say, like Shaunte and me, that you don't know who your mother is. Perhaps you haven't had a biological family to love, teach, and encourage you. Though you may not have a traditional, nuclear family, don't lose heart. You can have another kind of family — an eternal kind of family — that means more than any blood relation ever could.

Without a doubt, in your church and community, there are people asking "Who is my mother?" and "Who is my father?" Perhaps you know them. Perhaps you don't. But I encourage you to seek them out — and answer their questions with "I am." By taking responsibility for someone else's child — even if that child is no longer a child — you can be an instrument of hope and healing, a window to the love of the heavenly Father.

CHAPTER 8

The Seven Degrees of Transformation

Could everyone be connected by just a few people? A theory known as "The Six Degrees of Separation" — originally imagined by a Hungarian author and made popular by actor Kevin Bacon — states that each person is, on average, only six personal connections away from any other individual on earth.

Microsoft tested this theory with a digital experiment in 2007. Using a data set of instant messages made up of 30 billion conversations among 240 million people, the company found that the average path length among Microsoft Messenger users was 6.6. As a result of this experiment, some now refer to the theory as "The Seven Degrees of Separation."

How many connections does it take for someone to recognize his or her need for God? Toward the end of the "Jesus Movement," James Engel explored this idea in his book *What's Gone Wrong with the Harvest?* After taking a look at how people process their decision for Christ, he presents a theory, "The Engel Scale," which speculates that it takes a journey — a number of people and moments — before a person truly understands the Gospel, recognizes their need for God, and makes a life-changing commitment.

We can see this idea at work in 2 Kings 5. Naaman is a brave and valiant commander of the Syrian army. He's so highly regarded that, after an army raid, he is given a young girl from Israel to serve his wife as an indentured slave. Naaman is also quite sick with leprosy.

Connection 1: The young servant feels badly about Naaman's illness. "Boy, I wish my master could meet the prophet of Samaria," she says to her mistress in passing. "If he did, he would be healed of his skin disease."

Connection 2: Naaman's wife, who is also anxious for her husband to be healed, shares this information with him. "Honey, go get the prophet. *Now!*"

Connection 3: Naaman, willing to try anything, goes to get permission from his boss, King Hazael. Given that leprosy is contagious, the king is quite willing to let his army commander have some time off. "By all means, go get that taken care of," he answers. "In fact, I'll give you a letter of reference and the money to pay your way. Go talk to King Jehoram — he'll hook you up with the prophet."

Connection 4: Naaman pays a visit to King Jehoram and hands him the letter from King Hazael. The letter simply reads, *I have personally sent my commander to you so that you can heal him of his skin disease.*

King Hazael has forgotten to mention the prophet in the letter, and King Jehoram starts shredding his clothes like a crazy rock star. "Am I a god?" he wails. "Do you think I have the power to bring life and death? 'Heal this man?' Is that a joke? Hazael must be trying to start a fight — surely he knows I can't cure diseases!"

Connection 5: Elisha, the prophet, hears about King Jehoram's breakdown and sends a message. *No need to destroy the royal wardrobe. Send the man to me. I'll take care of his disease so that he'll know there is a prophet in Israel.*

King Jehoram calms down and gives Naaman directions to the prophet's house. Accompanied by an entourage complete with horses and chariots, Naaman arrives at Elisha's place. He seems to be under the impression that miracles are a red-carpet event, but Elisha doesn't even bother to come out and greet him.

Connection 6: Instead, Elisha sends his messenger, Gehazi, to speak with Naaman. "Go over there to the Jordan River," he instructs. "Dip, rinse, and repeat. Seriously — the 'repeat' part is important. Do it seven times, and you'll be as good as new."

Naaman is furious. Elisha has failed to meet his expectations. No personal greeting? No big spectacle? No major ritual prayer or sacrifice before his God? Just a dirty river? "If I wanted a bath," he whines, "there are better and cleaner rivers back home." Completely insulted, he stomps off.

Connection 7: Naaman's assistant runs after him. "What's the problem, boss? If he asked you to do something heroic and difficult, you would have done it gladly. Instead, he asked you to do something simple. Why refuse?"

Naaman, seeing his servant's point, sucks up his pride and goes swimming in the Jordan River. He dips seven times. *BAM!* His flesh is completely restored and looks even better than before.

Back at Elisha's place, Naaman declares, "I now know that there is no god but the God of Israel. Let me give you something to say 'thanks.'" Elisha refuses, standing his ground even as Naaman insists.

Naaman relents, but switches to another request. "Okay, then let me take a bunch of this dirt home as a memento, because I'm not going to worship any other god. And please — see that God forgives me when, as the army commander, I have to lend my arm to steady the king and end up bowing along with him."

Elisha grants Naaman's requests. "Everything will be all right," he says. "Go in peace."

Individually, none of these moments seem particularly significant. Each moment is so simple, so serendipitous. Each person plays his or her pivotal role — completely unaware of the bigger story that God is writing — and returns to the routines of regular life. No one person or moment would have been enough — it is God's orchestration of each of these people and each of these moments in sequence that result in a spectacular life-transformation.

My Seven Degrees

Like Naaman, my salvation story wasn't a star-studded, red-carpet event. It took more than one person to help me recognize the need I had for God. It took more than one moment for me to understand that life could be different with God. Measured separately, these moments are pretty mild. But measured together, as the organized effort of a God desperate to get a hold of my heart, these moments have transformed my life.

Connection 1: As an eight-year-old boy, I was invited to attend Vacation Bible School. The teachers — a bunch of church ladies — were simply nice to a young neighborhood boy. They didn't know what was going on in my home, and I wouldn't have even known how to explain it to them if I wanted to. Their kindness and love opened the door.

They told us the story of Jesus walking on the water and asked us if we wanted to meet Him. I figured He would walk through the door! I didn't fully understand what it meant to meet Jesus at that time — I wasn't ready. Though I always had a sense that God was watching over me, I didn't yet understand how that worked out in a personal way.

Connection 2: Stan Bratton, the man I shared about in the first chapter, gave me affirmation as we fixed my bike. Though Stan didn't become a Christian himself until the end of his life, God used his words to let me know that I wasn't invisible — I mattered. Stan's words — "You do that *well*" — also showed me that I didn't need to grow up to be like my parents. Their cycle didn't have to be my story.

Connection 3: I got a card from Larry Maddux, a Sunday school teacher. I had gone to his class once with a friend — we weren't attending church regularly at this time. The next Sunday, of course, I wasn't there. Later that week, I got a card from Larry that read, *We missed you at Sunday school.*

It was just something simple Larry did to show that he cared, but it truly left a mark on my heart. When I got that card, it told me that he knew I existed. It said that I was missed when I was gone. At the time, I didn't know that there was a follow-up program for Sunday school teachers or a system for tracking visitors. In my little-boy eyes, that card meant "Larry cares."

Connection 4: When I was around 15 years old, my mom decided we needed to start going back to church. My mom didn't force me to go with her, but I knew that it would make her happy. As I began attending, I was surprised to see that there were teenagers there — cute girls and other guys my age. It seemed great, so I continued to go with my mom each Sunday.

Mom was a link to a critical step in the journey for me. Her decision to go to church brought me to church too. That decision put me in an environment where I would hear from God and see godly role models. Without this connection, the final three connections wouldn't have been possible. I didn't know it at the time, but God had a lot more in store for me.

Connection 5: Not long after we started attending, one of the church ladies, Thelma Bartlett, came to "do a visitation." When she got to our apartment, I went to my room to let her and Mom talk. Through the door, I could hear Thelma tell Mom, "I think your son should go to Winter Camp with the youth group." My mom signed a check on the spot.

I was shocked. As soon as Thelma left, I asked Mom why she had signed me up. I did not want to go — I thought I might get brainwashed or something. Mom thought it would be good for me and figured that it might help me make some friends at the church.

Connection 6: On the way to Winter Camp, Tim Wilson asked me to sit next to him on the bus. Moments like these are often underestimated — it was a powerful gesture that God orchestrated to draw me to Himself. Tim's friendliness made me feel more comfortable. He showed me that these church kids really were just like me, and this allowed me to be open and receptive to what I would see and hear that very weekend.

Connection 7: While we were at Winter Camp, at first I just observed the youth group. Their authentic, exuberant worship intrigued me. I had never heard this kind of music or seen teens worshiping with hands raised before. I didn't understand, but it seemed like they knew God personally.

The next night, there was a wrestling in my soul. As I became more curious, I also became more agitated and uncomfortable. I found a spot under a table in the lodge area while the rest of the group was worshiping. I just started thinking out loud about all that I had witnessed that weekend — really praying to God.

Out of nowhere, this voice says, "If you give me your life, I'll be your Dad." I started crying. I couldn't pass up such a deal. I knew that my family was a disaster, and I felt like a disaster myself. I told God that I had nothing to give — I didn't think I was worth much — but that He could have my life.

Those students didn't know that they were modeling Christianity to me. It was very important for me to watch their lives — not only to realize that I needed God, but also to understand how I should live for God once I found Him. They became my new model to begin imitating what it meant to be "normal."

It took me seven connections to find God, but it doesn't always have to take that many. God can — and often does — perform miracles in just one of those moments. A friend of mine heard God speak to him at a Grateful Dead concert! Another friend committed his life to Christ after a near-death experience. The Apostle Paul certainly had a quick blinding-light-knocked-me-off-a-donkey conversion. Sometimes it just takes one. One instant. One person. One moment.

Transformation Through Royal Family KIDS Camp

Donni didn't have an easy life. Because of his parents' bad choices, he was placed in foster care. He went through a lot of foster homes, including several with moms and dads who genuinely loved him. Understandably, he was very sad and angry. He would get physically violent with his foster family, and even hurt himself. His behavior would spiral out of control, and the foster family would have no choice but to send him away.

When Donni was 10 years old, he attended Royal Family KIDS Camp. There, Counselors and Staff members talked to him about God. He didn't have a clear idea of what a real dad looked like or acted like, so it was difficult for him to wrap his mind around the idea of a heavenly Father. The Counselors explained that God would be better than an earthly dad — He would go with him everywhere, be his friend, protect him, forgive him, and love him.

At Camp that year, while he was supposed to be asleep, he asked Jesus into his heart.

Making Connections

Where are you in your journey toward Christ? Perhaps you're just discovering Him. Perhaps you're trying to figure Him out. Perhaps you're interested in what you've seen so far. Perhaps you've made a decision for Christ recently. Perhaps you've been a follower of His for quite some time. Wherever you are, recognize the beauty of the journey. God has orchestrated people, places, and moments — just the right ones, in just the right order — because He desperately wants to get a hold of *your* heart.

There are no small moments in the plans of God. Those seemingly routine activities — mentioning something in passing or sending a "thank you" card — might be a connection on someone's journey. Make it your goal to utilize each action, each moment, whether it seems significant or not, as an opportunity to point those around you toward the life-transforming love of God.

The Kingdom Dream

I'm not living the "American Dream." I'm living the "Kingdom Dream."

I didn't begin to fully comprehend and appreciate my own story until I began working at the national offices of Royal Family KIDS in 2003. As part of my job, I traveled the country, speaking to church

77

congregations, and enlisting them to reach out to children of abuse, abandonment, and neglect in their communities through Camps designed specifically for them.

In order to speak to these congregations effectively, I began to put together various Bible stories, recollections from my own life, and testimonies of some of the children we are privileged to serve. I never imagined that, by telling Royal Family stories, I'd also be digging up stories of my own. Reflecting on the heartbreaking backgrounds of those children — missed birthdays, drunk parents, and terrifying abuse — the similarities to my life's personal history compelled me to take a big-picture look at my own life.

As I did this, the black holes of my past filled in — fragmented memories and aspects of my childhood that I had locked away. After living with hazy recollections for decades, it was horrifying to recall and relive these painful scenes.

But even though I did begin to remember my hurts, I also began to see God revealing Himself as a Redeemer. Just as God, through one week of Camp, is able to reach out to the children of abuse and neglect at Royal Family, He also reached out to me through various moments and people in my life. With the added context of the redemption stories in the Bible, I had the message I wanted to share in a series of sermons: the hope of life-transformation.

Though the stories you have read in this book are saddening and painful at points, they are ultimately about hope. These stories are about God's love, and its power which breaks vicious cycles and transforms lives. There are certainly heartrending "befores" to each story, but — by the never-failing grace of God — there are also "afters" worth rejoicing over, too.

I am reminded through Bible stories, my own story, and the

children's stories — *God's life-stories are very long.* When we look back, we can see His hand of grace working in every trial, joy, triumph, challenge, and season. And, thankfully, the work of God's love doesn't end when this book does! God is still calling us to be used as instruments of life-transformation. Even though the children who attend Royal Family KIDS Camp leave with a better understanding of love than when they came, they don't go home perfect. They continue to go through the process of life-transformation long after their weeks at Camp are over — long after their childhoods are over. Their journeys continue. It's wonderful and amazing to see how children who have come through our Camps *return as adults* — to be positive examples of hope to other children in desperate need!

Nathan, who was serving in the Army overseas, received a special birthday surprise from his uncle, Wayne Tesch. Along with a gift, Wayne threw in some other "goodies" — including a bag of Royal Family KIDS purple and white M&M's. Nathan got a kick out of his uncle's thoughtfulness.

As Nathan ate his M&M's, a fellow Army buddy, Amber, approached him and asked how he had gotten purple and white ones. Nathan told her that his uncle, who worked with Royal Family KIDS Camps, had sent them.

"Royal Family KIDS Camp?" she asked incredulously. "I went to Royal Family KIDS Camp in Lancaster, California. That was one of the best weeks of my entire childhood!"

Amber went on to tell Nathan that, when she got out of the Army and returned to civilian life, she wanted to serve with Royal Family KIDS in some way. She was still being transformed and healed herself, but she felt the call to be an influence of life-transformation and an instrument of God's healing for others.

The same is true for me. I'm different from who I could have been, but I'm still far from perfect. God continues the process of transforming me, but He's willing to work on me and through me at the same time. From close to the beginning of the ministry of Royal Family KIDS, I've been able to volunteer, direct a Camp, and be a part of this incredible Royal Family. Now, as Vice President of Camps, I spend almost every day listening, laughing, crying, and celebrating with some of whom I feel are the most influential leaders in Christianity — our Camp Directors. We give ourselves away to the fatherless. We enlist and engage adults to love and to care. Together, we confront child abuse and change lives.

Not only am I transforming, but I'm also used by God as a transformer. I'm a paradox — I don't make sense. I've come from bad stock, but I'm producing good fruit. I don't feel like a miracle, but I know that I am. This life-transformation isn't something I can take any credit for — I haven't done anything. Rather, God has done the transforming in me and through me. I don't deserve what I have, what I get to do for a living, or my eternal destination. I'm not living the "American Dream." I'm living the "Kingdom Dream."

Wherever you are in your life today, I hope that these stories have encouraged your heart. Despite the different backgrounds we all may have, I believe that these stories are applicable to each of us. As sinful people, none of us are exempt from the need for God to extend His mercy and save us from ourselves. As redeemed people, none of us are exempt from God's life-transforming love and power in our lives. And as God's people, we are all called by Him to aid others on their journeys of transformation.

May we all be paradoxes — transforming, but also transformers. Though we have our sinful, broken pasts, may we, with God's daily help and strength, produce good fruit. May we become the parents of the parentless. May we live for those moments when we can be giant-slayers. May we relinquish that "third guy kind of thinking" in favor of being mindful to center our lives carrying out the eternal work of God's Kingdom. May we remember that moments, big or small, do matter ... perhaps more than we can ever know in this life. May we live not for the "American Dream," but for the "Kingdom Dream," one precious child at a time.

Glenn's Family

Stan's House

Glenn and Robin dating, college years

Glenn with RFKC grandparents, Darlene and Wilbur Mendell

Glenn's city baseball team

Glenn before being adopted

Glenn Garvin
Speaker

A current and clear communicator, Glenn tells it like it is. His multi-generational message of hope speaks to children, students, and parents alike. He inspires them to rise above their pasts and create new paths — not just for themselves, but for their families, friends, and churches.

Children and Youth of Abuse	Group homes, orphanages, Camps, Clubs, and small groups
Non-Profits	Raising support, technology, leading volunteers, and training
Christian Business Groups	Conflict management, leadership, and social networking
Colleges	Sociology, psychology, social action, and leadership
Conferences	Men, students, family, adoption, children of foster care, and Camps
Small Groups	Sunday school classes, mid-week small groups, and home groups
Churches	Sermons or mission's windows (1, 3, 5, or 10 minutes)

Interested in having Glenn speak to your group?

For more information,
visit www.RoyalFamilyKIDS.org or www.Hopebroker.com

Or contact him through:

Royal Family KIDS
3000 W. MacArthur Blvd, Suite 412
Santa Ana, CA 92704
(714) 438-2494

Royal Family KIDS email:
GlennG@RoyalFamilyKIDS.org

Personal email:
Glenn@Hopebroker.com

How wonderful to read stories of hope and transformation amidst encounters of abuse! While sharing vulnerably of his personal history, Glenn helps the reader better understand the trauma of abuse.

Biblical passages are viewed through another lens, and all the while, we are both encouraged and challenged to respond. This book is moving, challenging, inspiring, thought-provoking, and hope-giving.

Becca C. Johnson, Ph.D.
Licensed Psychologist
RFK Camp Director
Author, Speaker, Trainer, Psychologist, Author of *For Their Sake; Good Guilt, Bad Guilt; Overcoming Emotions that Destroy* (with Chip Ingram)

Glenn's life story is a story of healing, hope, and triumph. He has reached out to thousands of children to help them experience the love of God. His example of a humble, dedicated, Christ-like servant of God has put a smile on the faces of children who thought they may never smile again. Glenn's ministry to children can best be described by how James writes about the life of Abraham: "... Abraham believed God, and God counted him as righteous because of his faith. He was even called the friend of God" (James 2:23, NLT). This book is an amazing testimony of God's faithfulness and a beautiful story of how His grace is woven through the tapestry of a life. You will be encouraged and challenged reading it.

Rich Guerra
Southern California District
Assemblies of God Superintendent

I do not cry. Despite many years of hearing the saddest stories of helpless little victims of abuse, I never cry. I have experienced so much pain, and have absorbed the terror and hurt of so many others, that I didn't think I had any more tears in me. Then I read *A Seed of Hope in Toxic Soil*.

Glenn only alludes to the depth of the terror and the pain of the experiences, but having lived it, I read between those lines — and my stomach clenched up. Suddenly, surprisingly, my eyes were leaking. But rather than leave me there, Glenn, The Giant Killer, led me gently to a hope-filled place and left me with a smile and an encouragement to strive to live The Kingdom Dream.

Glenn, you are a Purveyor of Hope. You did this well.

Rhonda Sciortino
Author, Speaker, Real Estate Investor, Foster Care Advocate
Author of *Succeed Because of What You've Been Through*

I met Glenn years ago when he joined Royal Family KIDS, to work alongside Wayne Tesch, one of my great friends and colleagues. Glenn's life story has intrigued me on many levels. As I think about the significant challenges he had to face, the enormous obstacles he had to overcome ... the physical pain, the emotional trauma, the unanswered questions of his heart, the issues of his faith he had to wrestle with ... I'm once again in awe of the never-failing grace of God. I'm amazed and inspired at how God rescued this young man and used these very same life experiences to empower him to reach out to abused, abandoned, and neglected children today. I am sure that as you read *A Seed of Hope in Toxic Soil*, you'll come to realize those things too. To God be the glory, for the things He has done!

E. Dale Berkey
Co-Founder, President
BBS & Associates